THE GREAT BOOK OF ANIMAL KNOWLEDGE

# STARFISH

Colorful Wonders Under the Sea

All Rights Reserved. All content in this book may NOT be reproduced in any form or by any means, including scanning, photocopying, or otherwise without prior written permission from the copyright holder. Copyright © 2024 Gazelle Children's Books

# Introduction

Starfish, also known as sea stars, are fascinating marine animals found in oceans worldwide. They belong to a group called echinoderms, which means "spiny-skinned." Starfish are known for their unique appearance and ability to regenerate lost arms. Join us as we dive in and learn more about these amazing creatures.

# What Starfish Look Like

Starfish, also known as sea stars, are fascinating marine animals found in oceans worldwide. They belong to a group called echinoderms, which means "spiny-skinned." Starfish are known for their unique appearance and ability to regenerate lost arms.

# Incredible Diversity

There are about 2,000 species of starfish, each with unique characteristics. Some live in shallow waters, while others thrive in the deep sea. This diversity allows starfish to inhabit various marine environments, from coral reefs to sandy ocean floors.

# Size and Weight

Starfish vary in size and weight, ranging from less than an inch to over three feet in diameter. Most species weigh less than a pound, but larger ones can weigh up to eleven pounds. Their size often depends on their habitat and diet.

# Are Starfish Fish?

Despite their name, starfish are not fish. They lack a backbone and gills, which are characteristic of fish. Instead, starfish are echinoderms, closely related to sea urchins and sand dollars. They move using tiny tube feet located on their underside.

# Where Starfish Live

Starfish inhabit oceans all over the world. They can be found on rocky shores, coral reefs, sandy bottoms, and even in deep-sea environments. Their diverse habitats help them adapt to various oceanic conditions and thrive in different ecosystems.

# Where Starfish Sleep

Starfish don't sleep like humans. Instead, they have periods of rest where they become less active. They don't have a specific place to rest and can settle anywhere in their habitat, often clinging to rocks or hiding in crevices.

# How Starfish Move

Starfish move using hundreds of tiny tube feet located on their underside. These tube feet operate through hydraulic pressure, allowing the starfish to grip surfaces and propel themselves slowly across the ocean floor.

# Speed

Starfish are generally slow movers. They travel at an average speed of about 6 inches per minute. This slow pace is enough for them to search for food and find suitable spots to rest or hide from predators.

# Lifespan

The lifespan of a starfish varies by species. Most starfish live for about five to ten years, but some can live up to 35 years in the wild. Their ability to regenerate lost limbs contributes to their longevity.

# What Starfish Eat

Starfish are carnivores and primarily feed on mollusks like clams, oysters, and snails. Some species also eat small fish, coral, and plankton. Their diet helps control the population of these organisms in their habitat.

# How Starfish Eat

Starfish have a unique way of eating. They can push their stomachs out of their bodies and into their prey's shell to digest it externally. Once the prey is broken down, the starfish retracts its stomach and absorbs the nutrients.

# Are Starfish Blind?

Starfish are not completely blind. They have simple eyespots at the tips of their arms that detect light and dark, but they cannot see detailed images. These eyespots help them navigate and find food in their environment.

# Communication

Starfish communicate through chemical signals released into the water. These signals help them find food, identify mates, and warn each other of danger. They also use their sense of touch to interact with their surroundings and other starfish.

# Breeding Behavior

Starfish reproduce by releasing eggs and sperm into the water, where fertilization occurs externally. Most starfish species are broadcast spawners, releasing millions of eggs to increase the chances of successful fertilization and survival of their offspring.

# Mating Behavior

During the mating season, starfish gather in groups to increase the likelihood of fertilization. They align their bodies and release their reproductive cells simultaneously. Some species can also reproduce asexually by regenerating lost arms, which develop into new starfish.

# Baby Starfish

Baby starfish, or larvae, are tiny and look very different from adults. They float in the ocean as plankton before settling on the ocean floor and developing into the familiar star shape. This transformation is called metamorphosis.

# Predators

Starfish have several predators, including fish, sea otters, birds, and crabs. Their predators vary depending on their habitat. To protect themselves, starfish rely on their tough, spiny skin and ability to regenerate lost limbs.

# Warding Off Threats

To ward off threats, starfish use their hard, spiny skin as a defense mechanism. Some species can also release toxins to deter predators. Additionally, starfish can shed an arm to escape, which will eventually regenerate.

# Salty Secret

Starfish have a special ability to regulate salt within their bodies. They use a system of canals called the water vascular system, which helps them move and maintain balance in the salty ocean environment, ensuring their survival.

# A Tricky Relationship

Starfish have a complex relationship with coral reefs. While some starfish species help control the population of coral-eating organisms, others, like the crown-of-thorns starfish, can damage coral reefs by consuming large amounts of coral.

# Ocean Friends

Starfish thrive best in their natural ocean habitats, where they interact with various marine creatures like fish, crabs, and sea urchins. As pets, starfish often struggle to get the right conditions and diet, making them difficult to keep healthy.

# Starfish Shapes

Starfish are known for their star-shaped bodies, usually with five arms. However, some species have more arms, ranging from six to forty. Their shapes help them move efficiently and access food in various marine environments.

# Regenerative Abilities

Starfish have remarkable regenerative abilities. If they lose an arm, they can grow it back over time. Some species can even regenerate an entire starfish from a single arm, allowing them to survive and thrive despite injuries or predation.

For more information about our books, discounts, and updates, please Like us on Facebook!

Facebook.com/GazelleCB

Made in United States
North Haven, CT
12 August 2024